MARCH

Ellen Jackson

Illustrated by **Kay Life**

ini Charlesbridge

To my wonderful agent, Andrea Brown
—E. J.

With deepest friendship and love to the O'Gradys
In loving memory of Muzz and Gramps
—K. L.

Did You Know?

March is an anything-can-happen month. It is a month of change, of frost and overcoats, of kite flying and crocuses.

An old folk saying states that March comes in like a lion and goes out like a lamb. At the beginning of the month, winter winds bluster and blow, shredding clouds and whipping rain against windowpanes. But by the end of March, the sweet scent of spring is in the air.

The winds of March are perfect for kite fliers of all ages. Brightly colored kites shaped like dragons, flags, and fish bounce and weave in the pale blue sky. Children haul their kites down at dinnertime, but some remain behind, flapping in the branches of trees.

March is a time for spring-cleaning. Just as the winds of March sweep winter away, people sweep cobwebs out of their closets and attics. Even honeybees clean out their nests. Some bees have died during the icy winter, and the survivors drag the dead bodies to the entrance of the hive and push them out the front door.

Winter-weary children long to be outdoors in March. Spring fever is in the air, and animals, as well as people, feel it. Woodchucks and squirrels frequently move their babies to new nests or burrows to get away from the growing numbers of fleas and mites. Rabbits, too, seem restless and excitable in March because it is the beginning of their mating season. You may have heard the expression "mad as a March hare." This saying describes the agitation rabbits feel at this time of year.

The shamrock, a kind of clover, is a symbol for this green time of year. It is the national plant of Ireland, and on March 17, Saint Patrick's Day, many people wear shamrocks. Children sometimes hunt for a four-leafed shamrock among the three-leafed plants. Finding one is said to bring good luck.

The March Birthstone

The birthstone for March is the aquamarine. This gem ranges in color from deep blue to seawater green. According to legend, sirens once kept aquamarines in jeweled caskets at the bottom of the sea, but some of these precious stones eventually washed ashore. The Romans believed the aquamarine was sacred to Neptune, the god who ruled the oceans.

The March Flower

If you were born in March, your special flower is the daffodil, one of the first flowers to bloom in the spring. The daffodil has always been a symbol of life and new hope. Today some organizations sell daffodils to help fight cancer and other diseases.

Pisces

The March Zodiac

Pisces, the fish, is the astrological sign for people with birthdays from February 19 to March 20. People born under Pisces are said to have great imaginations and to love attention. They always see the good in people. For this reason, they are sometimes too forgiving. A Pisces is also thought to be a good storyteller and a good dancer.

The sign for people born from March 21 to April 19, is Aries, the ram. Those born under Aries are said to be bold, courageous, and energetic— the qualities of the ram. They may get angry easily but are also quick to forgive. An Aries is usually affectionate and enjoys finding new ways of doing things.

Aries

The Calendar

March is the third month of the year and has thirty-one days. It is named after Mars, the Roman god of war, crops, and vegetation.

For hundreds of years, March 21 marked the beginning of the new year in many parts of Europe. When March arrived, buds and tiny green leaves began to appear on trees. Flowers bloomed again, and the sun grew brighter. It was natural for people to think of the future and celebrate the new year during this time of warmth, growth, and rebirth. When Pope Gregory XIII introduced a new calendar in 1582, January 1 was made the beginning of the new year.

Sun, Sky, and Weather

March is an in-between month. It has no rules. Days are sometimes icy, sometimes warm. In March, the earth is damp with the melt of winter. Rain soaks plants and turns dirt into deep, squishy mud.

The winds of March toss tumbleweeds across the desert and flip clothes on clotheslines. Clouds dapple the meadow with sun and shadow.

The Anglo-Saxons, who settled in Britain in the fifth and sixth centuries, called March the loud and stormy month because of the frequent winds and rains. March winds are created when tropical air moves up from the equator and collides with polar air from the north.

Sunny days have a bite to them in March. Warm weather does not begin everywhere at the same time, but in many places the earth seems to wake up from a long sleep.

The moon is as high as the noontime sun in March, so this is a good time to observe it through binoculars. The March full moon has been called the worm moon by some Native American peoples of the Northeast because earthworms are often seen in early spring.

Animals in March

When the damp earth begins to warm in the sunshine, tiny tree frogs called spring peepers crawl out from under logs or from holes where they have spent the winter and begin to chirp.

Some insects hatch from eggs in early spring, while others come out of cocoons. Spring azures are one of the first butterflies to be seen in the woods.

Wood turtles can be found near ponds, streams, and puddles in March. When these turtles call for mates, they make a sound like a whistling teakettle.

Many birds fly south in the fall looking for warmer weather and a place where they can find food more easily. In the spring, they fly north again. The movement of animals and birds from one place to another with the change of seasons is called migration.

Robins, starlings, and red-winged blackbirds are some of the first birds to return north. Food is still scarce in March, but they can feed on withered berries, pill bugs, and spiders. The males search for nesting places that are close to a source of food.

Many mammals have been sleeping all winter. In March, some leave their dens with their young. Black bears bring their cubs outside for the first time.

You might see a mother opossum in March, but chances are you will not see her babies. These tiny animals are smaller than bees at birth. For the first two months, they never leave their mother's pouch.

The southwestern desert can be a pleasant place after the winter rains. A red-tailed hawk rides a warm wind above a rocky ridge. A cactus wren builds a nest in a nearby cholla. In the spring, verdins, thrashers, and other birds compete to build nests on the thorniest branches of chollas and cacti.

The first monarch butterflies return to the prairie with tattered wings and lay their eggs on milkweed plants in March. Monarchs that live to the east of the Rocky Mountains migrate thousands of miles to Mexico each year. No one knows how they find their way to Mexico and back to the prairie again. Perhaps they use the position of the stars or sun to navigate.

In the city, garter snakes appear in parks and grassy meadows. Squirrels scamper among neighborhood treetops, chewing at buds that are swollen with sap.

Plants in March

In the forest, pussy willows thrust their silver heads into the nippy air. The bare branches of hickories, elms, and oaks are lined with buds about to burst into flower. Wildflowers bloom early, before trees grow leaves that block out the flowers' sunlight.

In some parts of North America, skunk cabbage grows in the woods where the soil is wet. When a leaf is broken, this plant gives off a nasty smell similar to that of a real skunk. Even animals do not like the smell of this plant.

In March, the sap in sugar maple trees is flowing. People collect the sap and turn it into delicious sugar and syrup.

In the desert, plants such as jojoba and paloverde, cacti, grasses, and even some ferns and mosses look green and fresh. In later months, many of these plants will be dry and brown.

Lupines and poppies form patches of blue and gold on the hillsides if the winter rains have been heavy. These flowers will produce seeds while the weather is still mild. The seeds will be carried away by the wind or rain, or by animals and birds. When conditions are right, they will begin to grow in new places.

In Texas and Oklahoma, the prairie is splashed with blue, white, and yellow wildflowers such as sedges, anemones, bluets, and Johnny-jump-ups.

The first golden poppies bloom along the highways in California, and dandelions come up between the cracks in the sidewalks.

Special Days

Saint Patrick's Day

You have probably worn green on Saint Patrick's Day, but do you know who Saint Patrick was?

Patrick was born to a Roman family in Britain in the fifth century. At the age of sixteen, he was taken to Ireland by pirates and sold into slavery. Patrick worked herding pigs and cows for an Irish family. It was there he became dedicated to religion. Finally he escaped and returned to Britain. But he could not forget the Irish people.

Patrick returned to Ireland as a bishop and a missionary. He traveled throughout the land preaching to people and building churches, schools, and monasteries. Today he is the patron saint of Ireland, and he is honored on March 17.

Saint Patrick's Day is also celebrated in the United States. People sing Irish songs, dance Irish jigs, have parades, and make speeches wishing one another health and wealth. Shamrocks, green hats, and flags are everywhere. On Saint Patrick's Day, everyone wants to be part Irish and join in the fun.

The Equinox

You may have noticed that in the winter, afternoon shadows are dark and deep, and the sun sets quickly. When you get up in the morning, it may seem like the middle of the night! In the summer, the opposite is true. Daylight stretches into the evening hours, and the rosy colors of twilight linger in the sky.

But on two days of the year, all over the world, day and night are of equal length. One of these special days, called the spring equinox, occurs on or around March 20, when the sun is directly over the earth's equator. The word *equinox* comes from a Latin word that means "time of equal night." March 22 is usually the first day of spring in the Northern Hemisphere, which begins to warm up as it receives more and more direct sunlight. Summer is on its way.

Famous March Events

On March 15, 44 B.C., Julius Caesar was assassinated. He was a great general and leader who helped make Rome the center of a vast empire. Many Romans thought Caesar wanted to make himself king, even though he had refused the crown. A group of angry citizens led by Roman politicians Brutus and Cassius killed Caesar on the ides of March, the Roman name for March 15. For this reason, some people consider March 15 an unlucky day.

On March 13, 1781, Sir William Herschel discovered the planet Uranus using a telescope he had built himself. His sister, Caroline, gave him a great deal of help. She ground lenses for the telescope and made star maps for her brother. Uranus is the seventh planet from the sun.

Uranus

On March 10, 1876, Alexander Graham Bell spoke the first words over a telephone. He had been working on his invention for many months when he accidentally spilled some acid on his trousers. Without thinking, he shouted through the mouthpiece to his assistant, "Mr. Watson, come here! I want you." Watson came. The telephone had worked!

On March 27, 1964, a very strong earthquake shook Anchorage, Alaska. Buildings toppled over, and 115 people were killed. This earthquake caused a giant wall of water called a tsunami, or tidal wave, to rush toward the coast and batter the Alaskan cities of Valdez and Kodiak. A general store in Kodiak was carried out to sea. As the tide came in again, the store floated back and was left very close to its original location.

Birthdays

Many famous people were born in March.

Former Soviet political leader who helped bring new freedom to the Soviet people.

Inventor of the telephone, who also helped develop the phonograph.

Renaissance painter, sculptor, architect, and poet considered to be one of the greatest artists who ever lived.

Civil-rights leader and former mayor of Atlanta, Georgia.

Albert Einstein

March 14, 1879

Winner of the Nobel Prize for Physics. He discovered the theory of relativity.

Earl Warren

March 19, 1891

Fourteenth chief justice of the United States Supreme Court.

Gloria Steinem

March 25, 1934

Journalist and original publisher of *Ms.* magazine who is noted for her feminist views.

Sandra Day O'Conner

March 26, 1930

First woman to serve as justice of the United States Supreme Court.

Vincent van Gogh

March 30, 1853

Dutch painter known for his bold and powerful use of color and his post-Impressionist style.

Cesar Chavez

March 31, 1927

Labor leader who organized migrant farm workers to obtain better working conditions.

A March Myth

Old Winter sat alone in his cheerless wigwam. His hair was long and white and covered with frost.

Suddenly a beautiful maiden entered the wigwam. She wore a crown of violets, and her cloak was woven with grass and ferns.

The old man wondered at his strange visitor.

"I am Spring. She who walks among the flowers on a carpet of green," said the maiden. "The snow-cloth vanishes like darkness when I awaken the Great Fire from his long sleep."

Then the maiden touched the old man's cheek. His eyes closed, and he slept. Streams of water poured from his mouth.

The maiden stepped outside and walked across the plains, the hills, and the mountains. And where she walked, the flowers lifted their heads and greeted her with fragrance.

AUTHOR'S NOTE

This book gives an overview of the month of March in the Northern Hemisphere. But nature does not follow a strict schedule. The mating and migration of animals, the blooming of plants, and other natural events vary from year to year, or occur earlier or later in different places.

The zodiac sections of this book are included just for fun as part of the folklore of the month and should not be taken as accurate descriptions of any real people.

The March story was adapted from a story in *The Legends of the Iroquois* by William W. Canfield. (Port Washington: Ira J. Friedman, Inc. 1902.)

Text copyright © 2002 by Ellen Jackson
Illustrations copyright © 2002 by Kay Life
All rights reserved, including the right of
  reproduction in whole or in part in any form.

Published by Charlesbridge Publishing
85 Main Street, Watertown, MA 02472
(617) 926-0329
www.charlesbridge.com

Illustrations done in watercolor on Fabriano
  hot-press paper
Display type and text type set in Giovanni
Color separations made by Sung In Printing,
  South Korea
Printed and bound by Sung In Printing,
  South Korea
Production supervision by Brian G. Walker
Designed by Diane M. Earley

**Library of Congress
Cataloging-in-Publication Data**

Jackson, Ellen B., 1943-
   March/Ellen Jackson; illustrated by
Kay Life.
      p. cm.—(It happens in the month of)
   ISBN 0-88106-905-1 (hardcover)
   1. March (Month)—Folklore. 2. March
(Month)—Juvenile literature. [1. March
(Month)] I. Life, Kay, ill. II. Title.

GR930.J337   2002
398'.33—dc21   2001028269

Printed in South Korea
10 9 8 7 6 5 4 3 2 1